unhurried

A 52-Week Meditative Bible Reading Guide

Amy Jackson

Amy Jackson

From The Perch

Published by The Perch
31 W Downer Place, Suite 301
Aurora, IL 60506

www.theperchplace.com

info@theperchplace.com

The Perch provides space and skills for soul care so you can connect with God, yourself, and others in meaningful ways. We hold in-person and virtual retreats and workshops and offer soul care resources in our online store. See our website for more: www.theperchplace.com.

Cover and Interior Design: Jillian Hathaway
Cover Image: Image Source / Getty

ISBN 978-0-578-77965-2
Printed in the U.S.A.

For Jim

My biggest champion and cheerleader
I'm forever grateful that we're walking through life together.

introduction

On Friday, March 13, 2020, I walked to my daughter's elementary school to pick her up. As I waited for the bell to ring, I chatted with some of the other parents about the news of schools closing around the country due to a new coronavirus. We wondered aloud if our kids' school year would be cut short, exchanging worried glances as the students filed out of the building. We had no idea that within 48 hours our lives would be forever altered as one thing after another was postponed, called off, and closed. Life came to a sudden halt. Everything seemed to slow down.

In the coming weeks, people shared cute memes about "the great pause" and all the exciting things they planned to get done around the house while in quarantine. We joked about how nice it was to enjoy coffee on our couch in the morning and work in our pajamas. But when three weeks turned into three months without any end in sight, many of us realized that although we had less social plans, our lives were just as busy and hurried as before—perhaps more so.

The pandemic revealed our unhealthy relationship with busyness.

The pandemic revealed our unhealthy relationship with busyness. Some of us like to stay busy, rushing around, to prove our worth by our productivity. Some of us like to stay busy to avoid the discomfort of having to sit with ourselves. Many of us realized for the first time that the real busyness we feel isn't in our schedules, but in our hearts. Though our social lives came to a stop, our minds and hearts were as hurried as ever. And when we have difficulty slowing our hearts and minds, we have difficulty hearing from God.

This season has impressed on me the need to approach the Bible in an unhurried way, slowly meditating on a verse or two, allowing God to use the passage to transform me into the person I was created to be. When we approach Scripture in this slow, unhurried way, we will experience God's peace, love, and hope. We will better understand who we are and how God created us to live. We will learn to settle our minds and hearts, resting in God's love, no matter how chaotic the world around us may be. And, perhaps most importantly, we will train ourselves to listen for God's still, small voice.

This year has revealed to us that living an unhurried life has more to do with an inward peace than with an empty schedule. In these pages, I'll invite you to slowly, meditatively read the Bible, pondering it from multiple angles through various practices and exercises, all while listening for God's still, small voice. There's no need to rush here. You can take a deep breath and linger. Kick off your shoes, settle into your favorite chair, and enjoy some unhurried time with God.

Amy

Amy Jackson

how to use this guide

When we meditate on the Bible, we sit for a while with a verse or short passage, inviting God to speak to us. If you're unfamiliar with the term, meditating simply means to bring our full attention to something, turning it over in our minds, seeing it from different angles, and lingering with the words, phrases, and themes. I find that when I meditate on Scripture, it comes alive in new ways throughout my day. It comes up in a conversation I'm having or I read a similar sentiment in a book. I experience God speaking to me about the verse all day long in a million little ways. Meditative Bible reading is a simple yet rich practice that helps us hear from God.

As simple as meditative Bible reading is, it can be difficult to know where to start and even more difficult to keep it from feeling dull and rote. So this guide includes 52 weeks of meditative Bible reading exercises. You can start any day you choose. Nothing is dated, so this guide is ready whenever you are! I suggest starting on a Sunday or Monday to flow with the natural weekly rhythms of life.

Each week you'll find one Bible passage followed by a reflection prompt and five additional ways to engage the passage. On the first day of the week, you'll read the Bible passage and journal your answer to the reflection prompt in the space provided. Then each day for the remainder of the week, you'll read the same passage again, and then choose one of the other practices to continue engaging the Bible passage all week.

These varied practices can be done in any order. Together, they will help you meditate on the same Bible verse from multiple angles in multiple ways. Through these exercises, you'll gain deeper insights into who God is, who you are, and how you're called to live your life. You'll be invited to sit in God's presence, listen for God's voice, and rest in God's love.

This brings me to something you may have already realized: There are only six activities for each seven-day week. This is intentional. Part of slowing down and being unhurried is creating extra margin in our lives and schedules. On the seventh day of each week, you can take a break from the Bible reading, revisit one of the practices from that week, or come up with your own practice to engage the passage. As you become more comfortable with these ways of engaging the Bible, I sincerely hope you'll be inspired to come up with your own creative ideas, and you're welcome to use these ideas on the seventh day each week.

Before we begin, I want to make something abundantly clear: These activities aren't assignments. You aren't being graded. No one is watching to ensure you finish every practice each week. I genuinely believe you'll get so much out of each week if you do all six activities. But I want you to hear something loud and clear: The goal of this guide is not to give you homework to do each day; it's to invite you into God's presence in a deeper way. If you get to the end of the week and realize you only did three of the activities, there's no need to go back and finish the others. Turn the page without guilt and start on the next passage!

This guide isn't about seeking perfection but about opening ourselves to possibility. What does God want to say to you over the next 52 weeks? These practices are designed to help you slow your heart and mind enough to hear God's still, small voice.

how to make the most of this guide

The practices in this guide will deepen your relationship with God as they teach you to linger in God's presence. Remember: the goal is to cultivate an unhurried mind and heart so we can hear from God. To help you make the most of this guide, I offer these tips:

1. **Create a ritual.** Consider when and where you'll use this book each day. Maybe find a comfy space in your home that has meaningful art or objects. Maybe keep this book handy in the living room so that when you get a quiet moment during naptime you can easily find it. Maybe make this book part of your bedtime routine or your lunch break at work. This doesn't have to be permanent. After all, we know our schedules sometimes shift and change. But setting out with an intentional ritual can help make this practice especially grounding.

2. **Have a notebook nearby.** While there's space within these pages for reflection and jotting down notes, some of the practices invite more in-depth journaling and self-examination. Choose a dedicated notebook to accompany you on this journey.

3. **Make creative materials available.** You'll be invited to paint, doodle, draw, and sketch, so be sure you have plain paper and either watercolors, markers, or colored pencils wherever you'll be using this guide.

4. **Don't rush.** Let's be honest: you'll be tempted to hurry, to skip over, and to rush through. You may even be tempted to finish the book in less than 52 weeks. Resist the urge! Breathe deeply. Take your time. Graciously coax yourself to stop. Then start again.

5. **Go easy on yourself.** If engaging the Bible in this way is new, you may feel frustrated from time to time. That's okay! Take a deep breath, give yourself some grace, and then decide the best way to care for yourself that day. Maybe you need to do a different activity, repeat an activity you enjoyed, or just take a break for the day.

6. **Open yourself to possibility.** You'll most likely encounter activities and practices you're not familiar with. There's no need to be nervous or afraid. Explore why you feel anxious. Try out the practice. Then see how you feel afterward. You may find a new favorite way of connecting with God.

7. **Share what you're learning with a friend.** We were made for community. Even if you're using this guide on your own, regularly share with a friend, roommate, or significant other what you're hearing from God. Sharing with others is a fantastic way to process what you're learning.

8. **Remember God delights in you.** The God of the universe enjoys spending time with you. So feel free to linger and enjoy God's presence, knowing you are deeply, wholly, and unconditionally loved.

let's begin

When you call on me, when you come and pray to me, I'll listen. When you come looking for me, you'll find me. Yes, when you get serious about finding me and want it more than anything else, I'll make sure you won't be disappointed.

Jeremiah 29:12–13 (MSG)

As you embark on this journey, what's on your mind and heart? What is your prayer or hope? What are your concerns or questions?

- Pray a Conversational Prayer, speaking as you would to a friend. Tell God whatever is on your mind and heart, knowing that God hears every word and cares deeply for you.

- Create a timeline of your life with 10-year increments. For each decade, write 2-3 words to describe your relationship with God during that time. What are 2-3 words you'd use to describe your relationship with God right now? Then look at the timeline as a whole. What prayers, praises, or questions rise up as you look at your faith timeline?

- Write down the ways you're looking for God right now. Where and how do you tend to find God? If you feel like you've never really found God, why do you think that is?

- Listen to "Storyteller" by Morgan Harper Nichols. What stands out to you in the song? How does it relate to Jeremiah 29:12–13?

- Learn to listen the way God listens by working on your active listening skills as you listen to a friend or family member. This is an important way to show we care. Make eye contact, be fully present, listen to understand (not to respond), ask follow-up questions, try to empathize, and resist jumping to pat answers. Afterward, consider how easy or difficult it was for you to engage in active listening.

And may you have the power to understand, as all God's people should, how wide, how long, how high, and how deep his love is. May you experience the love of Christ, though it is too great to understand fully. Then you will be made complete with all the fullness of life and power that comes from God. *Ephesians 3:18–19 (NLT)*

When have you experienced the deep love of God? How did you experience it?

- Pray this passage as a prayer, personalizing it: "May I have the power to understand, as all God's people should, how wide, how long, how high, and how deep your love is. May I experience your love, though it is too great to understand fully. Then I will be made complete with all the fullness of life and power that comes from you. Amen."

- Pray this passage as a prayer for someone else, personalizing it: "May ________ have the power to understand, as all God's people should, how wide, how long, how high, and how deep your love is. May ________ experience your love, though it is too great to understand fully. God, make ________ complete with all the fullness of life and power that comes from you. Amen."

- Use *Lectio Divina* to sink deeper into this passage and notice what God wants you to see. (See appendix for instructions.)

- Practice Centering Prayer, focusing on the enormity of God's love as you simply rest in God's presence. (See appendix for instructions.)

- Paint, draw, sketch, or color as you meditate on this passage. When you think of the enormity of God's love, what images, colors, or words come to mind?

You'll welcome us with open arms when we run for cover to you. Let the party last all night! Stand guard over our celebration. You are famous, God, for welcoming God-seekers, for decking us out in delight. *Psalm 5:11–12 (MSG)*

Do you normally associate celebration with God? Why or why not? What in your life, big or small, might God be nudging you to celebrate today?

- Compare this passage to Luke 15:11-24. What do you notice? How do you feel knowing God welcomes us with open arms?

- Read the passage and notice which word stands out most to you. Use this word to focus your thoughts as you spend time in Listening Prayer. Quiet your mind and heart to sit quietly in God's presence and focus on this one word, listening for what God might have to say to you today.

- Make a list of your favorite ways to seek God. Which practices do you enjoy that connect you to God in meaningful ways? When and how do you connect most with God? What are you most often doing when you feel God speaking to you?

- Journal about a time when you felt God welcoming you with open arms, delighting in your presence. What were the circumstances? How were you feeling? In what ways did you feel God welcoming you with open arms? Include as many details as you can. Then read through what you've written and consider what God might be inviting you to notice.

- Consider who in your life needs to be welcomed with open arms. Who needs to be celebrated? Who needs to know they're not alone? Make a plan to meet this need this week.

Slow down. Take a deep breath. What's the hurry? Why wear yourself out? Just what are you after anyway?

Jeremiah 2:25 (MSG)

Would you say your average day is hurried or unhurried? Does your mind tend to feel hurried, busy, and rushed, or are you able to quiet your mind and heart?

- Practice mindfulness today by intentionally lingering during a normal activity, attempting to fully experience the moment. Mindfulness invites us to slow down and be fully present. For instance, you might spend time slowly drinking your coffee and savoring it, or you could extend your family dinner time to share a few extra stories or laughs. Other examples include taking the long way home from work, intentionally scheduling downtime between meetings, or giving your full attention to the person in front of you, whether a family member, friend, client, or coworker.

- Rest is ultimately an exercise in trust. We have to trust that God will take care of things while we take a break or sleep, believing that ultimately God is in control—not us. Intentionally spend time resting today and not being productive. You could take a break from work to zone out, leave a chore for the next day, take a nap, or even go to bed early.

- At the end of the day, spend time reflecting on when you felt the tug to be productive or the urge to hurry. Notice any patterns or triggers. Prayerfully consider how you may have missed God as you hurried through your day. Ask God to help you be more present and less hurried tomorrow.

- Journal: In what ways do you wear busyness and hurry as a badge of honor? What does your need to be productive tell you? How might your busyness be keeping you from addressing something important in your life or heart?

- Listen to "Not in a Hurry" by Will Reagan. What stands out to you in the song? How does it relate to Jeremiah 2:25?

WEEK 5

For you created my inmost being; you knit me together in my mother's womb. I praise you because I am fearfully and wonderfully made; your works are wonderful, I know that full well. *Psalm 139:13–14 (NIV)*

How do you feel about your physical health? How often do you consider your body and your physical health as related to your spiritual or soul health?

- God created our bodies to need rest daily and to need food multiple times a day. This wasn't an accident. Honor the way your body was created and choose one thing you will do today to take care of your physical health. It could be drinking more water, going for a long walk, eating more fruits and vegetables, taking a bike ride, stretching before bed, or getting more rest. Notice how taking care of your physical health impacts your mental, emotional, and spiritual health.

- Jesus regularly showed his disciples the importance of resting the body. See how many instances you can find of Jesus resting, talking about rest, or getting away to rest with his disciples. To get started, use BibleGateway.com to search "rest" in the Gospels: Matthew, Mark, Luke, and John.

- Consider all the inner workings of your body, all the unseen processes that work to keep your body moving and running smoothly. Thank God for the wonderful way your body is created.

- Write a thank-you note to your body for all that it can do (and has done) and all the ways it carries (and has carried) you.

- Engage Welcoming Prayer. (See appendix for instructions.)

The only thing that counts is faith expressing itself through love. *Galatians 5:6 (NIV)*

How would others say they see your faith expressed through love? How do you see others' faith expressed through love? Does faith expressing itself through love have to overtly mention God or faith? Why or why not?

- Use this simple Breath Prayer throughout your day. Breathe in as you pray, "Loving God," and breathe out as you pray, "Show me how to love today." Repeat for several moments as you breathe in and out.

- Meditate on the connection between faith and love. Why is it important that faith is expressed through love? Why do you think Paul writes that it's the only thing that counts? Is it possible to have true faith that doesn't express itself through love?

- Write out this verse and place it somewhere you'll see it often. Each time you encounter the verse, reflect on it.

- Choose at least one way you will show love to someone in your life today. Challenge yourself to think outside the box. Show love to someone in a new or unique way, or show love to someone outside your immediate family and close friends. Remember that the best way to show love to someone is to do something that feels loving to them. In other words, consider how they best receive love.

- Find a local organization or movement that is actively doing something that shows love to people in need. Determine today how you can support their work: through volunteering, financial gifts, or otherwise partnering with them.

She said to herself, "If I only touch his cloak, I will be healed." Jesus turned and saw her. "Take heart, daughter," he said, "your faith has healed you." And the woman was healed at that moment. *Matthew 9:21–22 (NIV)*

In what ways are you hungry for God's healing: physically, mentally, emotionally, spiritually, and/or relationally?

- Though the woman in the passage wasn't intending to be seen (in fact, she was used to going unseen in society), Jesus saw her. Not only that, he turned to see her, called her "daughter," and stated aloud for all around that she had been healed by faith. When have you felt seen by God?

- Consider the people you may overlook in life that Jesus sees. Who comes to mind? Pray: "Jesus, help me see the people that I tend to overlook, people you dearly love. Help me to see them through your eyes."

- Pray for anyone you know in need of healing: physically, mentally, emotionally, spiritually, and/or relationally. Pray also for your own healing.

- Read the fuller story in Luke 8:40–48. As you imagine what it would have been like to be the woman who was healed, sketch or color the scene. What do you think she was thinking and feeling? What do you think the people in the crowd thought and felt as they witnessed this scene?

- Practice Centering Prayer for at least five minutes (longer is even better!). Make the prayer of your heart: "If only I could be near him, I would be healed." Then spend time in God's presence. (See appendix for further instructions.)

WEEK 8

The light shines in the darkness, and the darkness has not overcome it. *John 1:5 (NLT)*

Knowing there is so much darkness in the world and in our lives, what questions, feelings, and thoughts come to mind as you read this passage?

- Use this modified Breath Prayer to focus on God's light, peace, and hope. As you breathe in, pray, "I breathe in your light," and as you breathe out, pray, "And I breathe out all the darkness in me." Then follow the same pattern for these Breath Prayers: "I breathe in your peace, and I breathe out all my worry and anxiety." "I breathe in your hope, and I breathe out my despair." Repeat as many times as you'd like. You might even create your own.

- Light a candle and then read this verse aloud at least three times, pausing between each reading. Then spend time in silent meditation on this verse as you look at the candle's light.

- Encourage someone in your life today. Who needs a reminder that no matter how dark life gets, the light of Jesus will always break through? You might write a card, send a text, set up a coffee date, or drop off a gift.

- Consider the places in your life where darkness seems to be winning out. Consider the places in your community where darkness seems to be winning out. How can you invite God's light into these places?

- Lament is ultimately an act of hope. It shows our hope that even in the darkness, we believe that things could be, should be, and will be better. Lament recognizes that God doesn't shy away from the darkness, and there's no need for us to pretend life isn't difficult. Spend time in lament today, speaking honestly about your anger, sadness, grief, and frustration.

I have hidden your word in my heart, that I might not sin against you. *Psalm 119:11 (NLT)*

Which Scripture verses have you memorized? When and why did you memorize them? What are your feelings and thoughts about memorizing Scripture?

- Journal: How have you been impacted by spending unhurried time in Scripture with this guide? How has it differed from other ways you've interacted with Scripture? What has been challenging for you? What has been beneficial?

- Commit this verse to memory so you can always remind yourself, no matter where you are, that spending time reflecting on Scripture is beneficial. Try reciting the verse several times a day or writing it down and putting it somewhere you can read it often.

- Divide a sheet of paper into four sections, labeling them: childhood, teenage years, adulthood, and today. Reflect on your relationship to the Bible in each period of life. Write or draw what comes to mind. For the "today" section, reflect on your relationship to the Bible in the past 6-12 months. As you look at the whole picture, what do you notice? Express your thoughts to God.

- Scripture can sometimes give us the words we need for prayer. This is definitely true of the Psalms, but there are so many Scripture passages that work well as prayers, especially the books written by Paul such as Ephesians and Philippians. Find a passage to pray either for yourself or someone else today. Not sure where to start? Revisit Ephesians 3:18–19 from Week 2, flip through the Psalms, or use Philippians 4:4–9 as a guide for praying for yourself or someone else.

- Write about a Scripture verse or passage that has been especially meaningful to you. What is the verse, and why is it meaningful to you?

WEEK 10

Therefore, since we are surrounded by such a huge crowd of witnesses to the life of faith, let us strip off every weight that slows us down, especially the sin that so easily trips us up. And let us run with endurance the race God has set before us. We do this by keeping our eyes on Jesus, the champion who initiates and perfects our faith. *Hebrews 12:1–2 (NLT)*

What holds you back from living the life God created you for? What helps you keep your eyes focused on Jesus?

- Use *Lectio Divina* to engage this passage. (See appendix for instructions.)

- Spend time running, walking, or otherwise being physical today as you meditate on this passage. What insights do you gain as you spend time doing an endurance activity?

- Confess to God those things that keep you from living the life you were created for. Write down the things, people, or situations that tend to distract you. Ask God for wisdom in overcoming anything that distracts you, trips you up, or steers you in the wrong direction. Ask for help in keeping your eyes focused on Jesus.

- Feats of endurance are often best done in community. We can encourage each other to keep going when the going gets tough. Reach out to a friend today to find a time to get together. Be sure to spend time listening to and encouraging your friend when you're together.

- Consider the people who have encouraged you to live your calling, to step out in faith, or to continue running the path marked out for you. How have they come alongside you to call out your gifts, remind you of your value, and/or mentor you? Thank God for these people today.

WEEK 11

True wisdom and power are found in God; counsel and understanding are his. *Job 12:13 (NLT)*

How do you typically gain wisdom and guidance from God? How do you seek it out? How does God speak to you?

- Use Free Journaling to see what God might have to say to you today. Set a timer for 5-10 minutes and grab a pen and paper or a journal. Respond to this prompt: "Right now I need wisdom for ..." Begin writing and don't stop until the time is up, writing down anything and everything that comes to mind, even if it doesn't seem related in the moment. When the time is up, read what you've written and note anything that stands out to you. What clarity did you gain?

- One of the ways God imparts wisdom is through the people in our lives. Friends, spiritual directors, counselors, and others can help point out important themes, share insights, and ask questions that bring us clarity. Consider how other people have helped you gain wisdom from God. How have you helped others in this way?

- James 1:5 reminds us that if we need wisdom, we only need to ask God for it. Spend time in prayer asking God for wisdom today.

- It's easy to get caught up seeking a detailed map rather than the Guide who walks with us along the path. Confess the ways uncertainty and the unknown weigh on you. Spend time expressing gratitude that even when we can't see the path ahead, the One who sees the whole trail walks with us and helps us navigate each step.

- Engage Welcoming Prayer. (See appendix for instructions.).

We are pressed on every side by troubles, but we are not crushed. We are perplexed, but not driven to despair. We are hunted down, but never abandoned by God. We get knocked down, but we are not destroyed. *2 Corinthians 4:8–9 (NLT)*

How do you tend to respond to challenges and adversity? In what ways is your response helpful and healthy? In what ways is it unhelpful and unhealthy?

- Journal about a time that you faced significant troubles in life. What were the circumstances? How did you react and respond? Looking back, how do you see God present during that time? How was the situation ultimately resolved? If it wasn't resolved, how were you able to move on despite it being unresolved?

- Consider the people who have supported you when life has gotten tough. How have they encouraged you to keep going? How have they helped carry you in difficult times? Thank God for the people in your life who have shown up for you and helped you live the life you're called to live.

- Listen to "Promises" by Antoine Bradford. What stands out to you in the song? How does it relate to 2 Corinthians 4:8-9?

- Come alongside someone who is currently facing troubles. How might you support, encourage, or provide for this person during this difficult season?

- Engage Labyrinth Prayer. Use the printed finger labyrinth in the appendix or find a walkable labyrinth near you. As you move toward the center of the labyrinth, reflect on the ways you currently feel discouraged or troubled. What is causing you frustration or turmoil right now? Once in the center, simply rest in God's presence. Hand over your worries, frustrations, and anxieties. When you're ready, follow the path out of the labyrinth, reminding yourself that no matter what you face in life, God walks alongside you every step, never abandoning you.

We ask God to give you complete knowledge of his will and to give you spiritual wisdom and understanding. Then the way you live will always honor and please the Lord, and your lives will produce every kind of good fruit. All the while, you will grow as you learn to know God better and better. *Colossians 1:9–10 (NLT)*

What are the practices that help you get to know God better and better? How often do you engage those practices?

- Pray for eyes to see how God is working in your life. As you go about your day, be mindful and pay attention to the ways God is present, nudging, working, inspiring, and convicting. At the end of the day, jot down any themes or moments that especially stand out to you.

- Reflect on the past 13 weeks spent with this guide. What fruit do you see God producing in your life? Thank God for the visible transformation.

- Take a quick assessment: How well are you honoring God with your life? Consider how you spend your time and money, honor the way your body was made, devote time to productivity and rest, treat others, live with purpose, and share God's love.

- Many times we're tempted to equate the way we speak to and treat ourselves with the way God speaks to and treats us. This can be detrimental. If we tend to be harsh critics, we may think God is critical of us as well. If we struggle to love ourselves, we may believe God does as well. That's why it's crucial to learn the truth about who God is. How do you tend to picture God in your mind? Sketch, color, or jot down words that represent how you see God. Then reflect: How does your view of God line up with the way Scripture describes God?

- Complete the inventory on the next page to reflect on the past 13 weeks.

pause

As you look back over the past 13 weeks, jot down what you're learning, contemplating, and wrestling with. Use these questions to guide you:

- What are you learning about God?

- What are you learning about yourself?

- What practices or activities are helping you feel connected to God?

- What new ways of engaging Scripture have been meaningful to you?

- What themes or recurring ideas have lingered with you?

- How has God been speaking to you?

WEEK 14

I pray that from his glorious, unlimited resources he will empower you with inner strength through his Spirit. Then Christ will make his home in your hearts as you trust in him. Your roots will grow down into God's love and keep you strong. *Ephesians 3:16–17 (NLT)*

Do you tend to have an abundance mindset or a scarcity mindset? In other words, do your actions show that you believe God has unlimited resources or that there's only so much to go around?

- Paint, color, or sketch a picture of a tree with roots going deep into the soil as you meditate on what it means for your roots to grow down into God's love.

- Use *Lectio Divina* to mull over this passage. (See appendix for instructions.)

- Pray this simple Breath Prayer (or create your own from this passage). Breathe in as you pray, "Loving God," and breathe out as you pray, "May my roots grow down deep into your love."

- Sit straight up in a chair with your feet firmly planted on the floor. Close your eyes and feel your bottom firmly in the chair, holding you. Feel your head lifting toward the ceiling with your back straight and tall. Feel your feet sink down into the floor, holding you steady. Imagine your feet sprouting roots that sink into the floor, into the ground, spreading deep and wide to anchor you, keeping you strong and steady. When you're ready, open your eyes and notice how grounded you feel. As you go about your day, notice when you feel rooted and grounded and when you don't. What contributes to these feelings?

- Write down three practices that help your roots grow down into God's love. Make a plan to engage one of these practices this week.

My command is this: Love each other as I have loved you.

John 15:12 (NIV)

What does it look like to love each other? How do others love you?

- Think through the Gospel accounts (the Books of Matthew, Mark, Luke, and John). If love is an action, how did Jesus love the disciples? Write down specific examples. What does this tell you about how you are to love others?

- Find one practical way to love someone outside your family today. What will you do to show your love?

- Think back to a time in your life when you felt God's love in a tangible way. Mentally place yourself back into that moment, remembering all the details with as many of your senses as possible. Then draw a picture that represents how you experienced God's love. Thank God for being present to you during that time.

- Engage Centering Prayer, placing yourself in God's presence to experience this great love firsthand. (See appendix for instructions.)

- God's love sets up an environment for us to thrive. Jesus modeled this well with his disciples. How can you be part of creating an environment where people thrive? Commit to doing something practical that will help create or further an environment of thriving for others. Possible ideas: Petition or march for legislation that helps people thrive, research and learn why people in your community aren't thriving to better understand the issues, or partner with a local organization that supports people on the margins of your community.

Jesus ... left in a boat to a remote area to be alone. But the crowds heard where he was headed and followed on foot from many towns. Jesus saw the huge crowd as he stepped from the boat, and he had compassion on them and healed their sick. *Matthew 14:13–14 (NLT)*

How do you respond to being alone? Do you enjoy the quiet solitude, or do you tend to avoid it? How much time do you spend in solitude on a regular basis?

- Use *Lectio Divina* to hear what God might have to say to you through this passage. (See appendix for instructions.)

- Jesus healed the people because upon seeing them, he was moved to compassion. Journal: When have you been moved to compassion? What moved you? Were you surprised that you were moved to compassion? What did you do as a result?

- Paint, doodle, sketch, or color as you meditate on this passage. What images, colors, or words come to mind?

- Use this Breath Prayer to align your heart with God's. Breathe in as you pray, "Compassionate God," and breathe out as you pray, "Break my heart with the things that break yours." Repeat this prayer as you breathe in and out. After you've spent several minutes doing this, notice what, if anything, has shifted in your heart and mind.

- How often do you see yourself as the person in the passage needing healing? List the ways you need healing today: physical, mental, emotional, relational, or spiritual. Pray a Conversational Prayer, boldly asking God to heal you in these specific ways.

It's impossible to please God apart from faith. And why? Because anyone who wants to approach God must believe both that he exists and that he cares enough to respond to those who seek him. *Hebrews 11:6 (MSG)*

Do you truly believe that God exists and cares enough to respond to you? Why or why not? Have you ever struggled to believe this?

- It's such a privilege that we are invited to go to God as a friend. Pray a Conversational Prayer today, simply talking to God about whatever is on your heart and mind.

- Journal: When have you doubted (or even wondered about) God's existence? What was that experience like for you? How did you deal with your doubt? What moved you from doubt to faith?

- Engage Labyrinth Prayer to reflect on your journey of faith. Use the printed labyrinth in the appendix to trace with your finger, or find a walkable labyrinth in your area. As you walk or move your finger toward the center of the labyrinth, consider: When have you felt far from God? When have you felt near God? Once you're in the middle of the labyrinth, simply rest in God's presence, enjoying the nearness. As you move back out of the labyrinth, ask God to allow you to take this feeling of nearness with you as you go about your day.

- Listen to "I Want Jesus to Walk with Me" by Sharon Irving. What stands out to you in this song? How does it relate to Hebrews 11:6?

- Search the word "faith" on BibleGateway.com. How many times does the word "faith" appear in the Bible? Browse through some of the verses that include the word "faith," especially in the Gospels (the Books of Matthew, Mark, Luke, and John). What insights do you gain about what faith looks like?

WEEK 18

Be still, and know that I am God. *Psalm 46:10 (NIV)*

How do you feel about being still and silent before God? Is it an enjoyable experience? Why or why not?

- Pray this verse as a Breath Prayer: Breathe in as you say, "Be still," and breathe out as you say, "and know that I am God." Breathe in and out for several minutes using this prayer. Notice what shifts in your heart and mind.

- Spend time in stillness meditating on this verse. Find a comfortable position, close your eyes, and simply be with God for at least 5 minutes.

- Plan or take a retreat where you can spend quiet time with God. It's ideal to have at least three hours away, but work with the time you've got. Even a short time away to be still, quiet, and focused on God is a blessing.

- Create a list of the things that are keeping your mind from being still today even if your body is still. When you're finished, hold up your list and pray this prayer: "God, I trust you with these worries. Give me wisdom and courage to take action in the ways you're leading me and to trust you with those things that are yours to take care of. Amen."

- Write out this verse on an index card along with the Bible reference. Then place the card somewhere you'll see it often: a mirror, your desk, or your car dashboard. Read it to yourself whenever you see it, committing this verse and reference to memory.

Because you are my helper, I sing for joy in the shadow of your wings. *Psalm 63:7 (NLT)*

How has God helped you? How has God come alongside you, fought for you, and supported you?

- Write your own psalm to express your feelings about God. Write a minimum of two lines. Then consider writing it on a sheet of paper and decorating it or typing it and printing it on nice paper. Prayerfully read your psalm to God.

- Listen to your favorite worship song and sing for joy. You might even choose to dance as you sing!

- The imagery used here is reminiscent of a mother hen gathering her chicks under her wings (see Matthew 23:37). It's a very motherly image, and it's one of the passages that highlights God's feminine qualities. Journal: How has God been motherly to you? How do you react to the idea of God being motherly? How might reflecting on the motherly aspects of God's character give us a fuller, richer understanding of who God is?

- Engage Centering Prayer as you focus on the fact that being in God's presence is like being safe under a mother bird's wings. Rest in God's protection and safety today. (See appendix for further instructions.)

- Get yourself comfortable. Wear comfortable clothing. Curl up in a favorite chair with a soft blanket, or relax in your bed. Brew a cup of your favorite coffee or tea. Listen to comforting, soothing music. Then read this verse aloud to yourself and meditate on the comfort you feel being under God's wings.

WEEK 20

For we are God's masterpiece. He has created us anew in Christ Jesus, so we can do the good things he planned for us long ago. *Ephesians 2:10 (NLT)*

How do you feel when you read this verse? What thoughts or questions arise? What images are brought to mind?

- *Visio Divina* is the practice of listening for God through art, images, or creation. Today, find a spiritual icon that's meaningful to you, go to an art display or museum, search online for a famous piece of art or an artist you're familiar with, or look at art that you have in your home. Simply sit and let God speak to you through the art. What do you notice? What comes to mind? What questions arise? Now consider: At what point was this art considered a masterpiece? When did the artist know it was complete? Is it possible the piece became a masterpiece before it was complete?

- Journal: In what ways do you struggle to believe you're a masterpiece? When have you felt that you're a mistake, a dud, or a failure? When have you felt stalled or useless? Now consider: How does God view you?

- Consider your calling or purpose in life. What has God put you on this earth to do? Ask God to make it clear to you.

- Create a piece of art that represents who you are and what your calling is. It could be a statement written in a lovely way, a collage of pictures of you with the people you love, a drawing of you living your calling, or simple images that represent who God created you to be.

- Whenever we find work that we truly enjoy, we can be tempted to hurry, hustle, and work non-stop. Spend time in prayer today exploring what it might look like to pursue your calling without being hurried.

If I had the gift of prophecy, and if I understood all of God's secret plans and possessed all knowledge, and if I had such faith that I could move mountains, but didn't love others, I would be nothing. If I gave everything I have to the poor and even sacrificed my body, I could boast about it; but if I didn't love others, I would have gained nothing. *1 Corinthians 13:2–3 (NLT)*

Who has loved you in a way that allowed you to see God through their actions? How does (or how did) this person love you in tangible ways?

- Listen to "Show Love" by Harper Still. What stands out to you in the song? How does it relate to 1 Corinthians 13:2–3?

- Paul is warning against the temptation to do important things, even for God, without loving people. Journal: Why do you think we're drawn to help other people, doing nice things for them, without truly loving them? How does this tendency show up in our service projects and mission trips? When have you been tempted to do this? Why is this a dangerous practice?

- Rewrite this passage in your own words. Use real life examples from today's world and from your culture. What insights did you gain from this activity?

- Determine one way you will show love to someone today. It could be someone in your family, a friend, a coworker, or someone else. Who will you show love to?

- Only when we receive God's love can we truly love others well. When we experience the deep love of God, allowing it to transform us from the inside out, we are compelled to share that love with others. Use this Breath Prayer to welcome God's love. Breathe in as you pray, "God, fill me with your love," and breathe out as you pray, "So that I can love others as you love me."

WEEK 22

For God has not given us a spirit of fear and timidity, but of power, love, and self-discipline. *2 Timothy 1:7 (NLT)*

When do you tend to be fearful or timid? Why? What would it look like to approach those situations with power, love, and self-discipline?

- Pray a Conversational Prayer, simply talking to God about your response to this verse. Share your thoughts and feelings with God openly, and listen for God's response.

- List the ways and the places you hold power. There may be clear, expected arenas like as a supervisor or a leader of a group. List also the ways and places that might not be as clear. For instance, you most likely have power in what you buy and from whom. You may have power in your community because of your gender or ethnicity. You may have power in what you teach your kids or in how you spend your time or in the work you do in your community. Once you've listed all the ways you hold power, consider how you use your power. How might God be inviting you to use your power?

- Find at least one way to use your power and voice to empower someone else today.

- Commit this verse to memory so you can always remind yourself of this truth, especially when you feel fearful or timid. Try reciting the verse several times a day or writing it down and putting it somewhere you can read it often.

- Engage Centering Prayer, intentionally placing yourself in God's presence, asking God to transform you into a person of power, love, and self-discipline. (See appendix for instructions.)

Even when I walk through the darkest valley, I will not be afraid, for you are close beside me. Your rod and your staff protect and comfort me. *Psalm 23:4 (NLT)*

When has God comforted you in the past? How have you experienced God's comfort—perhaps through other people, an inner peace, a safe place to process your situation, or a cozy bed?

- Use this Breath Prayer to meditate on this verse: Breathe in as you pray, "God of comfort," and breathe out as you pray, "Help me know you are near." Pray this as many times as you'd like. Then notice: How do you feel? What, if anything, has shifted in your heart and mind?

- Use *Lectio Divina* to engage this verse. (See appendix for instructions.)

- Talk to God in Conversational Prayer. Share the ways you're afraid, nervous, or anxious right now. Then listen for God's response. What does God have to say to you today?

- Consider the people in your life who need to be comforted. Then let your mind settle on one person in particular. What are some things that you could do to comfort this person? Determine one thing you will do today.

- Engage Labyrinth Prayer. Use the printed finger labyrinth in the appendix or find a walkable labyrinth near you. As you move toward the center of the labyrinth, reflect on the promise that God walks with us through life, no matter what we're facing. Once in the center, simply rest in God's presence, expressing thanks for God never leaving your side. When you're ready, follow the path out of the labyrinth, asking God to show you someone you can intentionally come alongside and encourage.

This, in essence, is the message we heard from Christ and are passing on to you: God is light, pure light; there's not a trace of darkness in him. *1 John 1:5 (MSG)*

What does it mean that "there's not a trace of darkness" in God? What might that mean practically? What might that mean for how you are to live your life in the light?

- Use this Breath Prayer to meditate on this verse. Breathe in as you pray, "God of light," and breathe out as you pray, "Light up every trace of darkness within me." Repeat as many times as you'd like. Then notice if anything has shifted within you.

- Pay attention to the light and shadows you encounter today. It might be the light and shadows on your desk, your own shadow on the ground, or the light from sunset streaming through the trees. What do you notice about the light? What do you notice about the shadows? Mindfully notice and allow yourself to wonder and ponder.

- Read *When God Made Light* by Matthew Paul Turner. Find the book at your local library, a bookstore, or search for it on YouTube to hear someone reading it aloud. How might God be speaking to you through this story? What insights do you gain as you read or listen to this story? What phrases particularly stand out to you?

- Listen to "Drive Out the Darkness" by The Porter's Gate. What stands out to you in the song? How does it relate to 1 John 1:5?

- Light a candle. Then paint, doodle, sketch, or color as you meditate on this verse today. What images, colors, or words come to mind?

WEEK 25

Search me, O God, and know my heart; test me and know my anxious thoughts. Point out anything in me that offends you, and lead me along the path of everlasting life. *Psalm 139:23–24 (NLT)*

How do you feel as you read this verse? What feelings and thoughts rise up in you at the thought of God searching your heart? Why?

- Read this passage aloud and then sit with your hands open, palms facing up, in a posture of receiving. Pray: "God, show me what you want me to see about myself today." Sit quietly, listening for God's still, small voice. What does God reveal to you as you listen? Jot down anything that comes to mind.

- Consider which tools have helped you understand yourself and your growing edges more clearly. Maybe you've used the Enneagram, an inventory, or an assessment. If no tool comes to mind, I highly suggest exploring the Enneagram. A great place to start is *The Road Back to You* by Ian Morgan Cron and Suzanne Stabile. Another great resource is The Enneagram Institute website.

- God doesn't search our hearts to bring us shame. You are loved and valuable no matter what! Journal: What parts of my past have brought me shame? What are the parts of myself that I don't like? Then consider: If God loves us and sees our value no matter what, what might God have to say to you in response to what you've written? Write as if God is writing to you.

- Engage Welcoming Prayer, welcoming God into every part of who you are. (See appendix for instructions.)

- Write this verse down and place it somewhere you can see it every day.

WEEK 26

I am leaving you with a gift—peace of mind and heart. And the peace I give is a gift the world cannot give. So don't be troubled or afraid. *John 14:27 (NLT)*

In what ways do you need the gift of peace of mind and heart today? What has you troubled or afraid?

- Engage Centering Prayer, spending time in God's presence, focusing on God's peace. (See appendix for instructions.)

- Listen to "Peace" by Sharon Irving. What stands out to you in the song? How does it relate to John 14:27?

- Use this Breath Prayer to focus on God's peace: Breathe in as you pray, "Gracious God" and breathe out as you pray, "I accept your peace." Breathe in and out, repeating this prayer, for several minutes. Notice how your mind, heart, and body relax as you rest in God's presence.

- Paint as you meditate on this verse. Watercolors are a perfect slow medium that naturally lends itself to meditation. As you paint, watch the colors swirl, blend, and bleed on the paper. Experiment using the paint on dry paper and then using your brush to get the paper a little wet first before adding the paint. Use colors that represent peace to you. Paint swatches, organic shapes, or a picture—whatever comes to mind. If you don't have watercolors, color and doodle with markers, pens, or crayons.

- Complete the inventory on the next page to reflect on the past 13 weeks.

pause

As you look back over the past 13 weeks, jot down what you're learning, contemplating, and wrestling with. Use these questions to guide you:

- What are you learning about God?

- What are you learning about yourself?

- What practices or activities are helping you feel connected to God?

- What new ways of engaging Scripture have been meaningful to you?

- What themes or recurring ideas have lingered with you?

- How has God been speaking to you?

Make every effort to add to your faith goodness; and to goodness, knowledge; and to knowledge, self-control; and to self-control, perseverance; and to perseverance, godliness; and to godliness, mutual affection; and to mutual affection, love. For if you possess these qualities in increasing measure, they will keep you from being ineffective and unproductive in your knowledge of our Lord Jesus Christ. *2 Peter 1:5–8 (NIV)*

What are your initial thoughts and feelings as you read this passage? What reservations or questions do you have?

- Use *Lectio Divina* to engage this passage. (See appendix for instructions.)

- Prayerfully consider this list: goodness, knowledge, self-control, perseverance, godliness, mutual affection, and love. Which do you see in your life? Which aren't as apparent? Ask God to show you one of these aspects that you can work on. Make a plan that invites you to receive from God and then act on it in some way.

- This verse warns against being "ineffective and unproductive in your knowledge of our Lord Jesus Christ." Spend 5-10 minutes Free Journaling your response to this question: What does it look like for you to be effective and productive in your knowledge of the Lord Jesus Christ? Set a timer and write until the timer goes off. Then read what you wrote and reflect on anything that stands out to you?

- Paint, doodle, sketch, or color as you meditate on this verse. What images, colors, or words come to mind?

- Create a Breath Prayer inspired by this passage that you can use throughout the day. A Breath Prayer is simply a one-sentence prayer that you tie to your inhalation and exhalation. Breathe in as you pray a name or image of God, and breathe out as you pray your desire or need. Repeat several times and use throughout your day anytime you have a short pause.

"When did we ever see you hungry and feed you, thirsty and give you a drink? And when did we ever see you sick or in prison and come to you?" Then the King will say, "I'm telling the solemn truth: Whenever you did one of these things to someone overlooked or ignored, that was me—you did it to me." *Matthew 25:38–40 (MSG)*

Who comes to mind when you read this passage? How do you see yourself in this passage?

- Meditate: How does living a hurried life make it easier to walk past or not even see those who are in need in your community? When has being hurried caused you to miss opportunities to be God's hands and feet? Pray that God would help you slow down enough to see these opportunities.

- Listen to "Hands and Feet" by The Brilliance. What stands out to you in the song? How does it relate to Matthew 25:38-40?

- Find at least one way to serve someone today. How might you practically serve someone who is often overlooked or ignored? Pay special attention to serving others in a way that defers to them, asking them what they need, rather than assuming you know what they need.

- Serve or support a local person or organization that is serving the hungry, sick, and/or imprisoned. If you're not sure who is doing this work locally, find out. Then determine a way to serve or support them.

- Journal: In what ways have you been overlooked or ignored? What was it like for you to be overlooked and ignored? Who has helped you feel seen? How have you felt seen by God?

We pray that you'll have the strength to stick it out over the long haul—not the grim strength of gritting your teeth but the glory-strength God gives. It is strength that endures the unendurable and spills over into joy, thanking the Father who makes us strong enough to take part in everything bright and beautiful that he has for us. *Colossians 1:11–12 (MSG)*

How do you tend to respond when you have to endure something you don't enjoy? What has helped you endure difficult situations?

- Use *Lectio Divina* to engage this passage. (See appendix for instructions.)

- Our bodies often show the stress we feel even before our minds recognize how stressed we are. Engage Welcoming Prayer to examine what your body might have to say to you today. (See appendix for instructions.)

- Journal: When have you persevered through a difficult time? Did you endure by gritting your teeth or through the "glory-strength" this passage talks about? How did God meet you in that season? Looking back, in what ways did God redeem that season?

- As you meditate on the theme of strength in this passage, paint, doodle, sketch, or write things that represent strength to you. How do these representations line up with this passage? What do you think God's idea of strength is?

- Who do you know in the midst of a difficult season? Use this passage as a guide to pray for this person: "I pray that ________ will have the strength to stick it out over the long haul—not by gritting their teeth, but with the glory-strength you give, God. Give ________ strength that endures the unendurable and spills over into joy. Amen."

Let all that I am wait quietly before God, for my hope is in him. He alone is my rock and my salvation, my fortress where I will not be shaken. *Psalm 62:5–6 (NLT)*

How do you respond when you have to wait? Does waiting tend to be difficult or easy for you?

- Meditate on your answer to this question: What is your response when you feel shaken? Ask God to show you. Do you respond with fear? Anger? Hurtful words? Distrust? Do you turn to prayer? Without feeling shame, ponder your response. What would it look like to respond with faith and hope when you feel shaken? Ask God to envelop you in love, a love that casts out all fear.

- Centering Prayer actively puts us in God's presence, quietly waiting for God to speak. Practice at least 5 minutes of Centering Prayer today. (See appendix for instructions.)

- Draw a large heart on a sheet of paper. Inside it, write or draw all the things that are weighing on your heart right now: worries, anxieties, things that break your heart, etc. When you're done, look at your heart. It's good for our hearts to be moved to compassion, moved to action over the needs of others, or even moved to anger over injustice. Jesus modeled all of these for us. Pray fervently, angrily, frustratingly for all these things today. Ask God to sort out for you which are yours to carry and which are God's to carry. Then notice if your heart is quieter and lighter.

- Use BibleGateway.com to search the Bible for other times the word "hope" is used. Browse through the verses to get a fuller picture of hope. What insights do you gain?

- Think back to a season of waiting in your life. As you look back, how did God meet you during that time? Journal your response.

WEEK 31

So Christ has truly set us free. Now make sure that you stay free, and don't get tied up again in slavery to the law. Galatians 5:1 (NLT)

What does it mean that you are set free? What are you free *from*? What are you free *for*?

- Do something today that makes you feel free. It could be doing a favorite hobby, going to a certain place, or being with a particular friend. Immerse yourself in the moment and enjoy.

- There is nothing you could do (or not do) that could make God love you any more or any less. Despite this, we are often tempted to add "musts" and "shoulds" to our spiritual lives. Examine: When have you fallen into this thinking? Why? How can you free yourself from this thinking?

- Use Free Journaling to help you hear from God. Set a timer for 5-10 minutes and grab a pen and paper or a journal. Respond to this prompt: "I try to earn or prove my value and worth by ..." Begin writing and don't stop until the time is up, writing down anything and everything that comes to mind. When the time is up, read what you've written. How is God speaking to you?

- One thing that can hold us back from freedom is having too much stuff. Identify one area of your home that needs some organization. Consider each item there and decide whether you want to keep it, donate it, or discard it. Once you've cut down on the number of items, you can organize the space. Notice how God speaks to you through this activity. What insights do you gain? How do you feel when you're done?

- In Galatians 5:16, Paul writes that the way to continue walking in freedom is to allow the Holy Spirit to guide our lives. Pray that the Spirit will guide you each day.

Because of the Lord's great love we are not consumed, for his compassions never fail. They are new every morning; great is your faithfulness. *Lamentations 3:22–23 (NIV)*

When have you struggled to believe that God loves you fully and unconditionally? When have you felt most loved by God?

- Meditate on God's great love for you as you paint, doodle, or color. What images, colors, or words come to mind?

- Get up early to enjoy the sunrise or find a picture of a sunrise. As you look at the sunrise, read the passage aloud. Then consider: What comfort do you gain knowing that God's compassions are new each morning, that God's faithfulness is true each day? As you look at the sunrise, still your heart and mind and listen for what God might be saying to you today.

- The context of this passage assumes that our troubles are sometimes so great that without God's great love we would be consumed. What are the troubles currently threatening to consume you? Pray about your troubles, giving them over to God, trusting that God's love can sustain you even in the most difficult circumstances. Pray that you will experience God's love today.

- Who has shown you love, especially when you've gone through difficult times? If you're able, reach out to connect and say thank you. If no one comes to mind, it's okay to grieve. Remember that no matter what, God deeply, wholly, and unconditionally loves you. Rest in this truth today.

- Write your own lamentation today, writing at least three lines. What are you lamenting? What are you asking God to do? Which of God's attributes or promises are you leaning on? Write out your lamentation and then read it aloud as a prayer.

Though your sins are like scarlet, they shall be as white as snow; though they are red as crimson, they shall be like wool. *Isaiah 1:18 (NIV)*

How often do you think about sin? What reactions or baggage do you have attached to the term? What feelings arise when you read this verse?

- Consider the things that keep you from God. What activities, habits, practices, or relationships make you feel distant from God? Why?

- We usually apply this verse to our own sins, but today remember that God sees all people as capable of being fully forgiven. Spend time in prayer reflecting on the people you tend to see as unforgiveable. Ask God to help you see these people through God's eyes.

- Listen to "I Have Made Mistakes" by The Oh Hellos. What stands out to you in the song? How does it relate to Isaiah 1:18?

- What sins do you need to confess to God today? Spend time confessing, knowing that God is quick to forgive. Then consider what you need to do to make things right with anyone who may have been hurt by your sin.

- Who do you need to forgive today? It could be someone who hurt you recently or a long time ago. Remember that the work of forgiveness is not dependent on the other person being sorry, available to talk, or willing to change. In addition, forgiveness does not require that you reach out to the person who hurt you or that you restore that relationship. Of course, if you feel God is inviting you to pursue reconciliation with that person, go for it!

God can do anything, you know—far more than you could ever imagine or guess or request in your wildest dreams! He does it not by pushing us around but by working within us, his Spirit deeply and gently within us. *Ephesians 3:20 (MSG)*

What dreams or wild hopes do you have? Which ones are so big or wild that you're afraid to even say out loud?

- Meditate on the work of the Holy Spirit. This verse reminds us that the Spirit works "deeply and gently within us." In what ways do you see the Spirit at work in your life? How do you see the Spirit working deeply and gently?

- Journal: When is it okay to be content *and* to long for things at the same time? For instance, can you be content with where you are in life and at the same time long for a deeper relationship with God? Can you be content with what God is doing in and through you and at the same time long for more of the Kingdom of God to be realized? When have you experienced both contentment and longing at the same time?

- This verse describes our partnership with God. Meditate on the idea of partnerships and how they differ from other kinds of working relationships. Paint, doodle, draw, or write your thoughts. What images come to mind?

- Pray a big, bold prayer today, trusting that God can do anything. How does it feel to pray like this?

- Engage Centering Prayer, allowing the Sprit to deeply and gently work within you. (See appendix for instructions.)

WEEK 35

You will know the truth, and the truth will set you free. *John 8:32 (NLT)*

How has the truth brought freedom in your life? How did you gain this truth?

- Meditate: When are you tempted to hide the truth, water down the truth, leave out the whole truth, or lie? What are the circumstances that make you hesitant to tell the truth (e.g., in conflict)?

- Journal: How has your life reflected the truth of this verse? Why is honesty the best policy? Why do you think truth-telling is so important to God?

- When we participate in justice work, we often are called to speak truth to leaders and groups that don't want to hear the truth. How might God be calling you to speak the truth today, even to people who may not want to hear it, in the name of justice and freedom? What will you do to obey?

- How do you tend to respond when you receive true but difficult feedback? Spend time in God's presence engaging Listening Prayer today, asking God to give you a clearer picture of yourself and the ways you're being invited to grow.

- Who in your life has permission to tell you the truth about yourself? How has this person helped you grow? Thank God for this person today and consider sending a thank-you note to this person. If you don't have someone like this in your life currently, who might be able to help you in this way?

The Lord replies, "I have seen violence done to the helpless, and I have heard the groans of the poor. Now I will rise up to rescue them, as they have longed for me to do." *Psalm 12:5 (NLT)*

Who do you think this verse speaks to today? Who are the helpless and poor that are crying out for rescue?

- Engage in Free Journaling to get your thoughts and feelings out. Set a timer for 5-10 minutes and grab a pen and paper or a journal. Respond to this prompt: "When I think about the justice of God, I ..." Begin writing and don't stop until the time is up, writing down anything and everything that comes to mind, even if it doesn't seem related in the moment. When the time is up, read what you've written and note anything that stands out to you. What did you learn about yourself? What might you need to explore further with God?

- Serve or support a local person or organization that is helping the helpless and/or poor in your community. If you're not sure who is doing this work locally, find out. Then determine a way to serve or support them.

- Spend time in lament today, crying out to God to rescue those who are experiencing violence and discrimination. Share your heart openly and pray big for God to rescue those in need.

- Sometimes in our pursuit of justice, we are tempted to believe it's all up to us—that we must do more, more, more! Confess the ways you've made justice work solely a human activity, pursuing it as if it were all up to you. Remind yourself that God is the One who brings justice, and we are invited to work alongside God in that pursuit.

- Journal: Which issue of justice is particularly close to your heart? Why? How does it reflect God's heart? How have you been involved in working for justice in this area?

WEEK 37

I tell you the truth, unless you turn from your sins and become like little children, you will never get into the Kingdom of Heaven. So anyone who becomes as humble as this little child is the greatest in the Kingdom of Heaven. *Matthew 18:3–4 (NLT)*

What do you think Jesus meant in this passage? What does it mean to become like little children?

- Humility is not thinking too much or too little of ourselves—it's seeing ourselves as God sees us. We are flawed and beautiful, weak and strong, lacking and worthy of more. Do you tend to think too much or too little of yourself? Meditate on this today, asking God to help you see yourself with true humility.

- Enjoy something that seems childish today. You could eat a favorite childhood treat, color or sketch, swing at the park, jump rope, or play a video game. Let your cares drift away as you play. Reflect: How does play help you connect with God? How does play help you connect with who God created you to be?

- Children have a wonderful way of making things simple and clear. What aspect of your faith feels complicated or complex? Pray that God would help you simplify your faith in this area.

- Engage Centering Prayer, knowing that God delights in time spent with you. (See appendix for instructions.)

- What is something in your life that you need to turn from? Confess this to God asking for forgiveness and guidance.

WEEK 38

When I am afraid, I will put my trust in you. *Psalm 56:3 (NLT)*

How often do you experience fear or anxiety? What tends to trigger these feelings in you?

- Engage Welcoming Prayer to notice how your body might be holding anxiety or stress. (See appendix for instructions.)

- Create a Breath Prayer you can use whenever you feel anxiety or fear. A Breath Prayer is simply a one-sentence prayer that you tie to your inhalation and exhalation. Breathe in as you pray a name or image of God, and breathe out as you pray your desire or need. Repeat several times and use throughout your day anytime you have a short pause. Here's one example: "God who sees me, I put my trust in you."

- Journal: What are your usual coping strategies when you face fear or anxiety? How healthy are they? How well do they work? How doable are they in your current season of life? Do you need to identify some new coping strategies?

- Listen to "Look Up Child" by Lauren Daigle. What stands out to you in the song? How does it relate to Psalm 56:3?

- Create a calming kit. Include pictures, mementos, a candle, quotes, or anything else that reminds you to breathe deeply and place your trust in God. You could display the items together on a shelf or side table, or you might keep them together in a box or drawer so you can pull them out whenever you need them. Consider writing out this verse on an index card to include in your calming kit.

The Spirit of God, the Master, is on me because God anointed me. He sent me to preach good news to the poor, heal the heartbroken, announce freedom to all captives, pardon all prisoners. God sent me to announce the year of his grace—a celebration of God's destruction of our enemies—and to comfort all who mourn. *Isaiah 61:1–2 (MSG)*

How is Jesus good news to you? What about Jesus initially drew you in? What draws you to Jesus now?

- In Luke 4, Jesus quotes this passage as his mission, and we are invited into this same mission. What might this look like practically in today's world? In what ways might God be inviting you into this mission today?

- Listen to "Let Us Be Known" by The Porter's Gate. What stands out to you in the song? How does it relate to Isaiah 61:1–2?

- Read this blessing over yourself as you touch the appropriate part of your body: "God, anoint me to carry out your mission here on earth, with everything I am. Make my eyes able to see you in every person I meet. Make my mouth a loud-speaker sharing your hope, peace, and love with the people in my life. Make my heart an overflowing stream of your lovingkindness, spilling out onto everyone I encounter. Make my hands instruments of healing as they touch, comfort, create, build, and hold. Make my feet strong and swift, carrying the good news of your grace and freedom. May my whole life partner with you in the work you're doing in this world."

- Pray for anyone in your life who needs God's peace, love, hope, and grace. Ask God how you might be good news to them.

- Complete the inventory on the next page to reflect on the past 13 weeks.

pause

As you look back over the past 13 weeks, jot down what you're learning, contemplating, and wrestling with. Use these questions to guide you:

- What are you learning about God?

- What are you learning about yourself?

- What practices or activities are helping you feel connected to God?

- What new ways of engaging Scripture have been meaningful to you?

- What themes or recurring ideas have lingered with you?

- How has God been speaking to you?

WEEK 40

Be on guard. Stand firm in the faith. Be courageous. Be strong. And do everything with love. *1 Corinthians 16:13–14 (NLT)*

How does this passage hit you today? In what ways did you need this passage today?

- Create a Breath Prayer to focus on one or two of the parts of this passage. Breathe in as you pray a name or image of God, and breathe out as you pray your desire. Here's one example: "God who has called me, help me be courageous."

- Commit this verse to memory. Try reciting the verse several times a day or writing it down and putting it somewhere you can read it often. Don't forget to include the reference.

- Paint, doodle, sketch, or color as you meditate on this passage. What images, colors, or words come to mind?

- Journal: How might living an unhurried life help you live out this verse? How might being more unhurried help you hear God's voice guiding you to be faithful, courageous, strong, and loving?

- Stand in front of a mirror for this embodied prayer. Cup your ears with your hands as if you're listening and say, "Be on guard." Plant your feet firmly on the floor and stretch the top of your head toward the ceiling so you're standing up straight and tall as you say, "Stand firm in the faith." Stand in a "superhero stance"—place your fists on your hips with your feet slightly apart—and say, "Be courageous." Put both arms up, flexing your muscles like a bodybuilder as you say, "Be strong." Last, put your hands over your heart and say, "And do everything with love. Amen."

WEEK 41

Yahweh! The Lord! The God of compassion and mercy! I am slow to anger and filled with unfailing love and faithfulness.

Exodus 34:6 (NLT)

When you think of God, what images or words come to mind? How do you view God?

- Journal: Think back to your childhood or when you were first told about God. What were you taught? What was your understanding? How did you view God? How has your view of God changed and evolved over time? What contributed to these changes? If it's helpful, you might draw or doodle the way you used to envision God next to the way you envision God today.

- Sometimes we believe our own critical inner voice is the voice of God, but this verse reminds us that God is compassionate, merciful, slow to anger, loving, and faithful. If this is who God is, what might God want to say to you today? Quiet yourself and listen for God's still, small voice. Then write a note to yourself as if God is writing.

- Engage Centering Prayer and spend time with our loving, compassionate, faithful God. (See appendix for instructions.)

- Meditate on the aspects of God mentioned in this verse. Which one appeals to you most during this season? Why?

- Reflect on the ways you've experienced God's compassion, mercy, love, and faithfulness. Spend time in prayer thanking God for being present and praising God for being full of compassion, mercy, love, and faithfulness.

WEEK 42

Live in me. Make your home in me just as I do in you. In the same way that a branch can't bear grapes by itself but only by being joined to the vine, you can't bear fruit unless you are joined with me. *John 15:4 (MSG)*

What might a metaphor about a plant with seasons of growth, harvest, and dormancy tell us about the fruit in our lives? How might it speak to being unhurried?

- Write down the activities or practices that help you to "make your home" in Jesus. How often do you spend time doing these activities?

- Engage *Visio Divina* to deepen your understanding of this verse. Visit a vineyard or find a picture of a vineyard and sit with the image for at least 15 minutes. Ask God to reveal truth to you as you look and ponder. Notice all the details. What insights do you gain?

- Check in with yourself with this simple form of Prayer of Examen, which is a way of recollecting the day. What fruit do you see in your life as a result of spending unhurried time with God? In what ways do you hope to see more fruit in your life? Pray about your responses, talking to God.

- This passage paints a picture of a partnership with God that results in our growth and transformation. Journal: If God produces the growth and transformation in your life, what is your role in this partnership? How does God ask you to join in?

- Enjoy a glass of wine. Each glass of wine tells a story of the particular grape on a particular vine grown in a particular place during particular weather by particular people. Reflect on all the particulars that have contributed to the wine you're enjoying. How does the fruit in your life similarly reflect the particular place, time, circumstances, and other factors in your life?

The fundamental fact of existence is that this trust in God, this faith, is the firm foundation under everything that makes life worth living. It's our handle on what we can't see. *Hebrews 11:1 (MSG)*

How does our faith serve as a firm foundation for our lives? How does it give us a handle on what we can't see?

- Sit comfortably, ensuring your feet are firmly on the floor. Close your eyes and feel your body sink heavy into the chair and floor. Feel the weight of your bottom on the seat and your feet on the floor. Notice how the chair and the floor hold you, creating a firm foundation that supports you. Now remember that our faith in God is the firm foundation under our lives, holding and supporting us. Breathe in and out slowly, allowing your body to release and rest, knowing that you are held.

- Use *Lectio Divina* to engage this verse. (See appendix for instructions.)

- Make a pie chart of the things that make your life worth living. Draw a circle and then create sections for the various things that bring your life meaning. The more meaning an item brings, the bigger its section should be. When you're done, take a look at your pie chart. What stands out to you? What surprises you?

- Journal: How do you feel about your faith right now? Does it feel strong, firm, and active? Does it feel lacking, or are there doubts? How does this lead you to pray right now?

- Consider the questions you have today that don't have answers. How do you respond to uncertainty and the unknown? How did you respond to the uncertainty of pandemic life? After reflecting on this, pray that God will help you see and also that you will trust God with all that you can't see.

They all ate as much as they wanted, and afterward, the disciples picked up twelve baskets of leftovers. About 5,000 men were fed that day, in addition to all the women and children! *Matthew 14:20–21 (NLT)*

What would you do differently if you lived as if there were more than enough resources, love, grace, and help to go around?

- In this story, Jesus honors the way our bodies are made and feeds the people—not just enough to tide them over, not just so they have a decent meal, but so that they all are satisfied, with more than enough. Determine one way you can honor your body today, giving it what it needs. It could be rest, water, nourishing foods, a long walk, or something else.

- Count your blessings today. Make a list of the ways that God is providing for your needs right now. What relationships, resources, love, grace, and help is God giving you right now? Thank God for providing for you.

- There are certainly times in our lives when we don't feel satisfied. You may even be in an unsatisfied season right now. Reflect on the ways you feel unsatisfied and ask God to help you feel content in this season, even as you long for more, trusting that God is more than able to provide all you need.

- Quietly do something generous today. You might provide in some way, give generously, or share your time generously. Do this to emulate our generous God, not for any recognition.

- Engage Welcoming Prayer, welcoming Jesus into every part of your body and life. (See appendix for instructions.)

All praise to God, the Father of our Lord Jesus Christ. God is our merciful Father and the source of all comfort. He comforts us in all our troubles so that we can comfort others. When they are troubled, we will be able to give them the same comfort God has given us. *2 Corinthians 1:3–4 (NLT)*

In what ways do you need God's comfort today? What troubles are you facing? What anxieties are occupying your mind?

- Use *Lectio Divina* to engage this verse. (See appendix for instructions.)

- Listen to "Mercy" by The Brilliance. What stands out to you in the song? How does it relate to 2 Corinthians 1:3–4?

- Use this Breath Prayer to meditate on this verse. Breathe in as you pray, "God of comfort," and breathe out as you pray, "Help me know you are near." Pray this as many times as you'd like. Then notice: How do you feel? What, if anything, has shifted in your mind and heart.

- Consider the people in your life who need to be comforted today. Then let your mind settle on one person in particular. Determine one thing you can do today to comfort this person. Remember to think of things the person would see as helpful, not necessarily what you would want if you were in their situation.

- Journal: How has going through a difficult time allowed you to comfort others who are going through hardship? When have you been able to use your experience to comfort someone else? How have others been able to comfort you because they had been through something similar?

WEEK 46

Therefore, if anyone is in Christ, the new creation has come: The old has gone, the new is here! *2 Corinthians 5:17 (NIV)*

Do you feel like a new creation? Why or why not? What does it look like to be a new creation in God?

- Search BibleGateway.com to see when the word "new" is used in the Bible. Browse through the verses, pausing with any that stand out to you. What picture do you gain about the ways God is making things new—including the ways God is making you new?

- Reflect on the ways that God has made you new over your life. How is God making you new in this season? Journal your responses and then thank God for all the work being done in your heart and mind making you a new creation.

- Spend time in prayer reflecting on the things in your life that are no longer serving you. What might you need to say goodbye to? Is there a relationship, a habit, a commitment, or an item (or collection of items) that God is inviting you to step away from? Ask God to direct you and give you courage to act.

- Identify something in your life that needs some new life injected into it. It could be an area of your home, a disorganized corner, your exercise routine, your morning commute, a relationship, or something else entirely. Make a plan for how you will bring new life to this area or item today.

- Meditate on the theme of new life. Paint, doodle, sketch, or draw whatever comes to mind. What images, colors, or words do you think of when you think of new life?

WEEK 47

So let's not get tired of doing what is good. At just the right time we will reap a harvest of blessing if we don't give up.

Galatians 6:9 (NLT)

In what ways are you feeling tired today? Are you feeling tired emotionally, spiritually, mentally, physically?

- One common lament is to ask, "God, how long?" In other words, how much longer until you break through, make things better, or change things? Spend some time lamenting today, asking, "God, how long must I wait? How long until you _______?"

- Listen to "Your Labor Is Not in Vain" by The Porter's Gate. What stands out to you in the song? How does it relate to Galatians 6:9?

- Journal: When have you seen a season of waiting give way to a season of harvest and blessing? How long were you waiting? What were you waiting for? How did the season of harvest line up with what you expected or hoped for? How did God show up?

- Make a list of the things that help you persevere in difficult seasons. Are there people, practices, or coping strategies that help you wait well?

- Meditate on this verse, thinking about how you tend to react to seasons of waiting. Allow your mind to wander back to various times in your life that required a lot of waiting. What makes waiting difficult or easy for you? How have you seen God show up in seasons of waiting?

WEEK 48

Then, because so many people were coming and going that they did not even have a chance to eat, he said to them, "Come with me by yourselves to a quiet place and get some rest." *Mark 6:31 (NIV)*

When do you find yourself addicted to busyness? What are the signs that you've become addicted to busyness?

- Jesus reminded the disciples to honor their bodies' needs. Honor the way your body was created and choose one thing you will do today to take care of your physical health. It could be drinking more water, going for a long walk, eating more fruits and vegetables, taking a bike ride, stretching before bed, or getting more rest. Notice how taking care of your physical health impacts your mental, emotional, and spiritual health.

- Meditate: How is God speaking to you about being unhurried? How might you bring a slower rhythm to the various areas of your life? Think about your home life, work life, social life, etc.

- Intentionally choose to do a task extra slowly today. Slowly read. Use a slow method to make your coffee, like pour over or French press. Pick the longest line at checkout. Or savor your meal, chewing each bite slowly. What insights do you gain by doing this task slowly today?

- Journal: What specific calling has God given you? What unique gifts, talents, personality, and experiences has God given you to live a life of purpose? How are you currently living out that calling? When have you found yourself so busy doing what you feel called to do that you fail to take care of your body, mind, and heart? Why might workaholism be extra tempting when we're doing something we feel called to do?

- Choose your favorite slow way to spend time with God today. Choose an idea from this guide or a practice you come up with. If possible, get away to a quiet place to do this activity today.

None of this fazes us because Jesus loves us. I'm absolutely convinced that nothing—nothing living or dead, angelic or demonic, today or tomorrow, high or low, thinkable or unthinkable—absolutely nothing can get between us and God's love because of the way that Jesus our Master has embraced us. *Romans 8:37–39 (MSG)*

Why is it important for us to understand that nothing can separate us from God's love? How does this knowledge free us to live differently?

- Use *Lectio Divina* to engage this passage. (See appendix for instructions.)
- Listen to "Nothing to Fear" by The Porter's Gate. What stands out to you in the song? How does it relate to Romans 8:37–39?
- Turn this passage into a prayer of praise. Pray: "Nothing fazes me because you love me. I'm absolutely convinced that nothing—nothing living or dead, angelic or demonic, today or tomorrow, high or low, thinkable or unthinkable—absolutely nothing can get between me and your love because of the way that you have embraced me. Thank you, God, for your amazing, unconditional, all-encompassing, never-ending love!"
- Meditate: How might understanding and experiencing this great love drive out our fear (1 John 4:18)? How do you most often experience God's love? How does experiencing God's love change your perspective on life?
- Engage Centering Prayer, placing yourself in God's loving presence. (See appendix for instructions.)

By his divine power, God has given us everything we need for living a godly life. We have received all of this by coming to know him, the one who called us to himself by means of his marvelous glory and excellence. *2 Peter 1:3 (NLT)*

How would you summarize what it means to live a godly life? How would you describe it to a child?

- Make a list of what you've been given to live a godly life. What gifts, skills, help, and support do you have? Thank God for all that you've been given so you can live the life you've been created for.

- Journal: In what ways do you struggle to live a godly life? Are there certain sins, habits, or routines that prevent you from living the life you were created for? Is there a theme or topic you need to learn more about? Is there an aspect of godly living that you feel uncomfortable with? When you're done journaling, use Conversational Prayer to speak openly to God about your struggles and concerns. Ask God for what you need.

- Meditate on who God is. What does God want to point out to you today? What insights do you gain?

- Paint, doodle, sketch, or color as you meditate on this verse. What does it look like to live a godly life? What images, colors, or words come to mind?

- In what specific ways is God calling you to live in this season? How is God inviting you to step more fully into your calling? Take action today or make a plan to take action this week.

My counsel for you is simple and straightforward: Just go ahead with what you've been given. You received Christ Jesus, the Master; now live him. You're deeply rooted in him. You're well constructed upon him. You know your way around the faith. Now do what you've been taught. School's out; quit studying the subject and start living it! And let your living spill over into thanksgiving. *Colossians 2:6–7 (MSG)*

What does it look like to "live Jesus"? What would your life look like if you were living Jesus every day?

- Meditate on the ways you feel deeply rooted in Jesus. What contributes to you feeling deeply rooted?

- Use *Lectio Divina* to engage this passage. (See appendix for instructions.)

- How is God speaking to you about taking action? In what way(s) might God be inviting you to do something in response to what you've been learning? Take action today or make a plan to take action this week.

- Stand tall with your feet firmly planted on the floor and your arms resting at your sides. Close your eyes and imagine your feet growing roots that shoot down deep into the ground and hold you steady. Thank God for anchoring you with love. Now imagine yourself as a large, well-constructed building. Thank God for the ways you've been built up, tall and strong. Finally, picture yourself in a graduation cap and gown. Thank God for all you've learned about God, about yourself, and about living the life you were created for. Even though there is still more growing to do, even though there are still additions for the building, even though there is still more learning to do, thank God for all you've been given to live a godly life.

- As you reflect back on your journey with this guide, what are you grateful for? Express your thanks to God.

There has never been the slightest doubt in my mind that the God who started this great work in you would keep at it and bring it to a flourishing finish on the very day Christ Jesus appears. *Philippians 1:6 (MSG)*

What would it look like for you to be flourishing? What would a flourishing life feel like?

- Complete the inventory on the next page to reflect on the past 13 weeks.

- Take a look back at all four of the Pause inventories you've filled out. Journal: As you reflect back on this journey of meditative Bible reading, what stands out to you? What is the work that God has been doing in your heart and mind? Where do you see growth? What work is still in process? What are the ideas or themes you're still pondering?

- What are your favorite ways of connecting with God? How does God most often speak to you? Moving forward, how will you create space for regularly connecting with God? Make a plan that fits your life.

- Use Labyrinth Prayer to reflect on the journey you've been on with this guide. Use the printed finger labyrinth in the appendix or find a walkable labyrinth near you. As you follow the path toward the center, reflect on the ways God has been present during this journey. What has God been showing you? Telling you? Once you're in the center, pause and simply rest in God's presence. When you're ready, follow the path back out, inviting God to continue working in your life, and asking for what you need as you continue on in life.

- Make space for celebration today! How will you celebrate completing this guide and all the work God has been doing in your mind and heart?

pause

As you look back over the past 13 weeks, jot down what you're learning, contemplating, and wrestling with. Use these questions to guide you:

- What are you learning about God?

- What are you learning about yourself?

- What practices or activities are helping you feel connected to God?

- What new ways of engaging Scripture have been meaningful to you?

- What themes or recurring ideas have lingered with you?

- How has God been speaking to you?

appendix

lectio divina

Lectio Divina is an ancient practice used by Christians to engage Scripture. It invites us to listen for how God is speaking to us through a passage of Scripture in this very moment. It's best to use a very short passage or a single verse of the Bible, like the passages for each week in this guide. To get started, settle yourself internally by taking a few deep breaths in and out and mentally preparing yourself to hear from God.

Read the passage aloud to yourself, listening for any word or phrase that stands out to you. Then pause for several minutes of silence, allowing God to direct you to a word or phrase.

Read the passage aloud again. This time as you read, meditate on your word or phrase, listening for what God might have to say to you through this word or phrase. Pause for silence after you've read.

Read the passage a third time, meditating on how God might be inviting you to respond today. Pause for several minutes of silence to allow yourself time to listen for what God is saying to you.

Finally, spend time silently enjoying God's presence. When you're done, take a deep breath in and out before you move on with the rest of your day. Keep a look out for ways God might continue to speak to you throughout the day. I often find my word or phrase continuing to pop up throughout the rest of my day.

centering prayer

Centering Prayer is as simple as spending time in God's presence in silent prayer—and that can be incredibly difficult to do! This type of prayer is based on the belief that we're transformed when we spend time in God's presence. So Centering Prayer invites us to intentionally place ourselves in God's presence, listening for God's still, small voice rather than bringing our own words, thoughts, or agendas. There's no performance, fancy words, or formula here, which is what can make it challenging for many of us.

Because it doesn't feel like we're doing much in this type of prayer, you may wonder if it's beneficial. Centering Prayer asks that we trust that God will bring the change without any of our own striving. You may or may not feel any different after engaging Centering Prayer, but over time, you will see the effects of spending this time in God's presence.

Find a comfortable position that you can stay in for several minutes undisturbed. To get started, I recommend choosing a word of intention from the Bible passage for the week. This word can help keep you focused on listening to God. Whenever your mind wanders, simply bring it back to your chosen word. This is the work of Centering Prayer: bringing your focus back to God when your mind wanders. It's natural for this to happen, and it will wander less the more you practice. Whenever your mind wanders or you get distracted, gently bring your focus back to your word. Do this as many times as you need to without any guilt or shame. Here's a tip: Sometimes I have a thought that keeps distracting me that I don't want to forget—like something I really need from the grocery store. I like to keep a notepad nearby so I can jot these things down and stop focusing on them.

Set a timer for your desired amount of time so that you won't be distracted thinking about how long you've been praying. When the timer goes off, take one more deep breath in and out, and then draw yourself back to the present moment. If you're new to Centering Prayer, I suggest starting with five minutes. As you get more comfortable, you can spend 10, 20, or even 30 minutes in this meditative prayer.

welcoming prayer

Welcoming Prayer purposely draws our attention to our body and helps us listen for the ways God is speaking through our whole selves. During this prayer, we're invited to welcome Jesus into every aspect of who we are.

Find a comfortable position that you can stay in for several minutes. This prayer works really well lying down, but you can also sit comfortably in a chair or cross-legged on the floor. Next you'll begin scanning your body. Starting with your toes and moving to your head, mentally scan your entire body, noticing any tension, pain, or other sensations. Reflect on each area of tension without judgment and pray, "Welcome, Jesus," as you breathe and try to let go of the tension. To further help me connect to my body, I often gently touch the area of tension as I do this. Reflect: What might God be pointing out to you as you scan your body? How might God be speaking to you through any tension or pain you're experiencing?

Once you've completed your body scan, sit quietly with Jesus for at least one minute. Welcome Jesus into every part of your life, body, circumstances, and relationships. Finish your time by praying, "I let go of my need to be in control, and I welcome you, Jesus, to lead in every part of my life, body, circumstances, and relationships. Amen."

APPENDIX

labyrinth prayer

Labyrinth Prayer was created as a slow, meditative way to reflect on your life as a sacred journey. It uses a labyrinth—a winding path that leads you toward the center and then back out again—to help you connect your body to your reflections and thoughts. This practice can mimic the spiritual practice of pilgrimage, and it's much more accessible. You can find walkable labyrinths where the path is often marked with bricks or stones. Finger labyrinths are also available in many shapes, sizes, and materials so that people can engage Labyrinth Prayer anywhere. At The Perch, I offer six-inch carved bamboo labyrinths to people at our workshops and retreats to trace with a stylus.

If you're able to find a walkable labyrinth near you, I highly suggest trying it out. Labyrinth Prayer is especially meaningful when you get to physically move your body. If that's not an option, you can use the printed labyrinth on the next page wherever you are! Use your finger, a capped pen, or the eraser end of a pencil to slowly trace the path. To be clear, in a labyrinth, the path only leads one way. You can't get lost—it's not a maze. As you trace the path toward the center, reflect on your life as a sacred journey. In the center, rest in God's presence. Then, as you follow the path back out, ask God for whatever you need for the rest of your day, such as peace, endurance, or wisdom.

The Perch provides space and skills for soul care. We're located in Aurora, Illinois, and we'd love to have you join us for an in-person event. No matter where you live, though, I hope you'll follow us on Facebook and Instagram, join us for a virtual event, and shop our online store.

Visit us online: www.theperchplace.com
Follow us on social media: @theperchplace

We'd love to hear about your experience with *Unhurried*. Use the hashtag #unhurriedbook when you post on social media, and email us your stories: info@theperchplace.com.